FIRST 50
BACH PIECES

YOU SHOULD PLAY ON PIANO

ISBN 978-1-7051-2477-2

Visit Hal Leonard Online at
www.halleonard.com

Contact Us:
Hal Leonard
7777 West Bluemound Road
Milwaukee, WI 53213
Email: info@halleonard.com

In Europe, contact:
Hal Leonard Europe Limited
1 Red Place
London, W1K 6PL
Email: info@halleonardeurope.com

In Australia, contact:
Hal Leonard Australia Pty. Ltd.
4 Lentara Court
Cheltenham, Victoria, 3192 Australia
Email: info@halleonard.com.au

CONTENTS

Air on the G String

from Orchestral Suite No. 3 in D Major, BWV 1068

Johann Sebastian Bach
arranged by Richard Walters

Aria
from *Goldberg Variations*, BWV 988

Johann Sebastian Bach
(1685–1750)

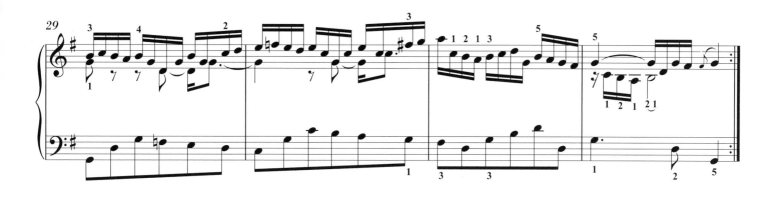

Arioso
from Cantata BWV 156

Johann Sebastian Bach
(1685–1750)

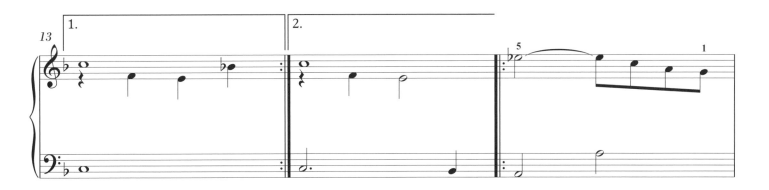

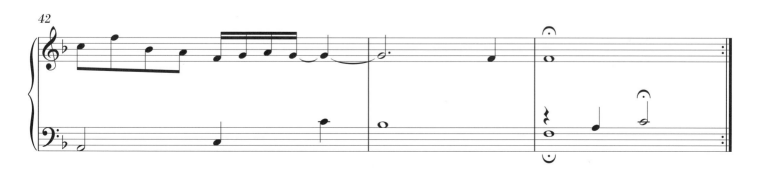

Badinerie
from Orchestral Suite No. 2, BWV 1067

Johann Sebastian Bach

Bourrée
from Lute Suite No. 1 in E minor, BWV 996

Johann Sebastian Bach

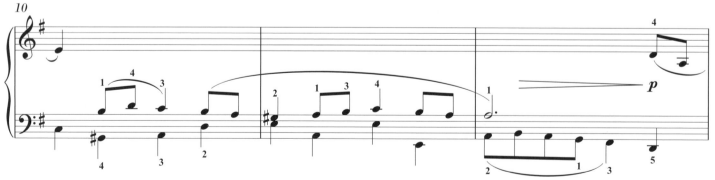

Chaconne
from Violin Partita No. 2 in D minor, BWV 1004

Johann Sebastian Bach

Andante maestoso, ma non troppo lento

Minuet
from Overture in F Major, BWV 820

Johann Sebastian Bach

* Play small notes second time.

Gavotte II
from English Suite No. 6 in D minor, BWV 811

Johann Sebastian Bach

* Alternate fingering is for the repeat.

Gavotte
from French Suite No. 5 in G Major, BWV 816

Johann Sebastian Bach

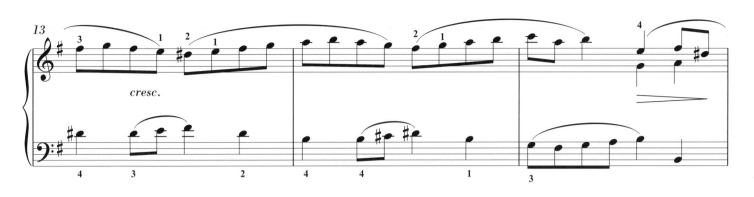

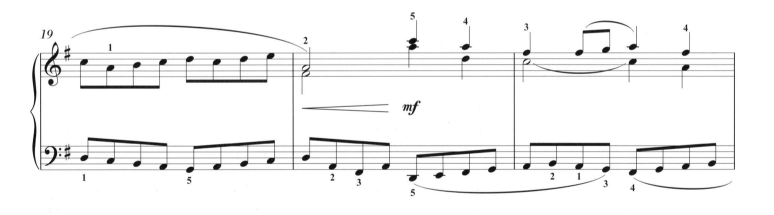

Gavotte en Rondeau
from Overture in G minor, BWV 822

Johann Sebastian Bach

Invention No. 1 in C Major
BWV 772

Johann Sebastian Bach

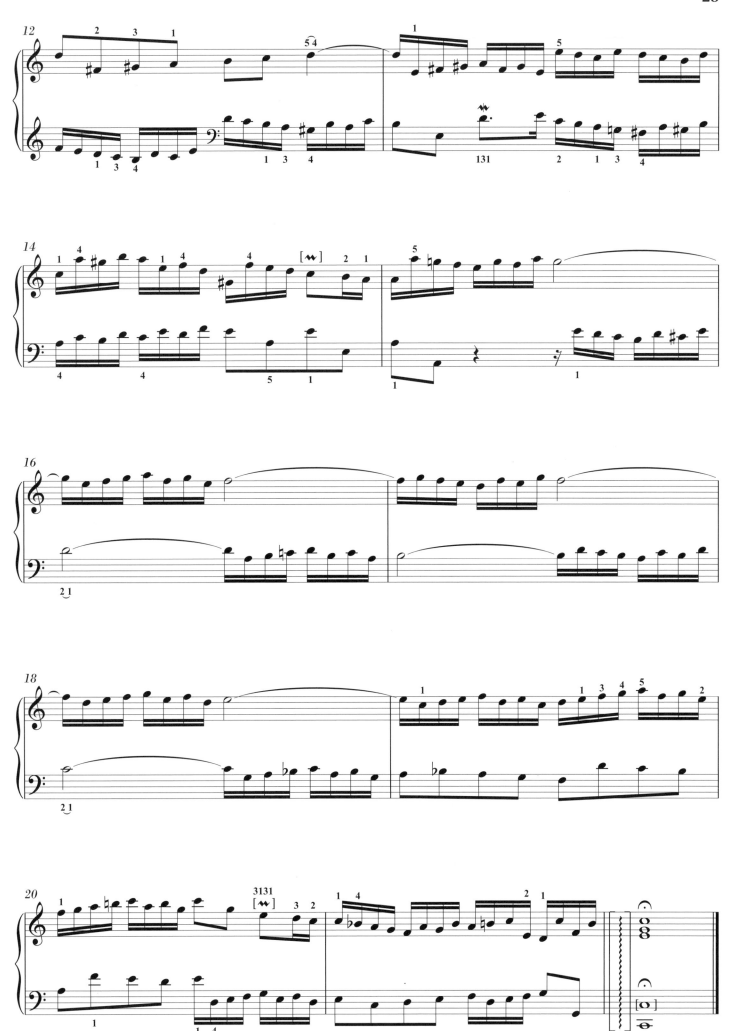

Invention No. 4 in D minor
BWV 775

Johann Sebastian Bach

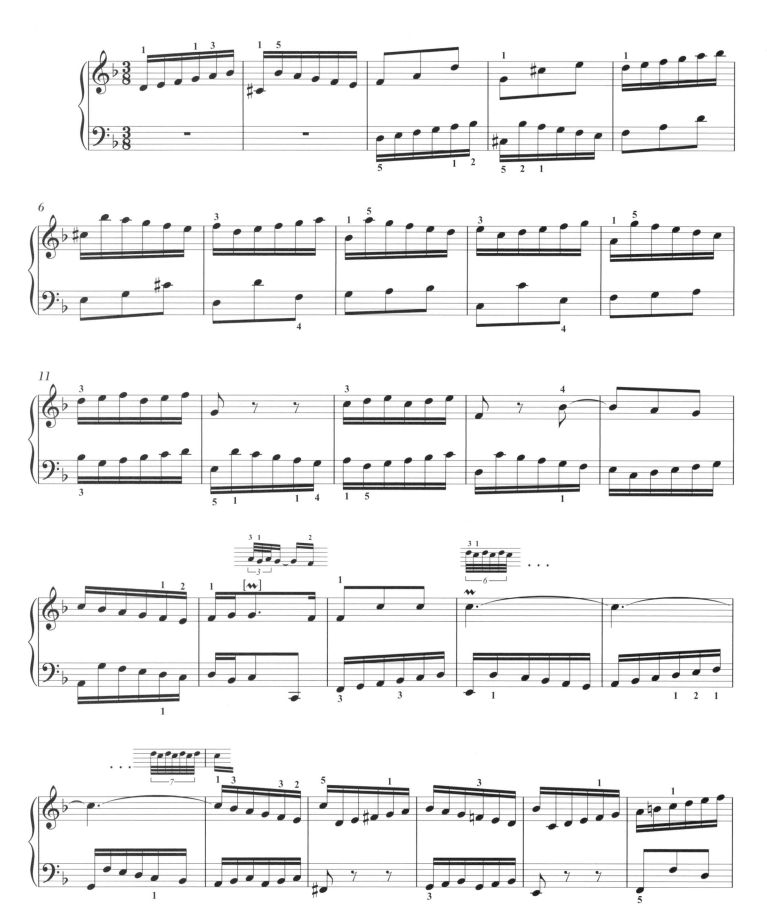

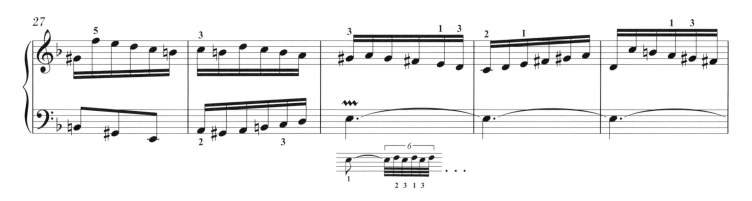

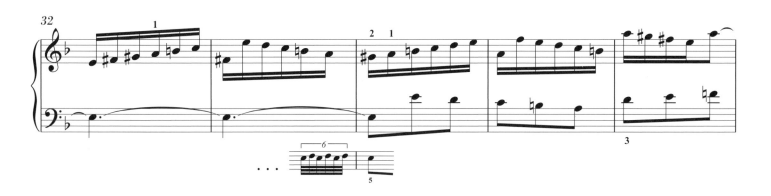

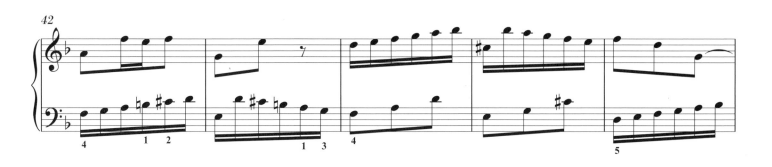

Invention No. 8 in F Major
BWV 779

Johann Sebastian Bach

Fingerings are editorial suggestions.

Invention No. 10 in G Major
BWV 781

Johann Sebastian Bach

Invention No. 15 in B minor
BWV 786

Johann Sebastian Bach

Jesu, Joy of Man's Desiring

Johann Sebastian Bach

March in E-flat Major
BWV Appendix 127

Johann Sebastian Bach

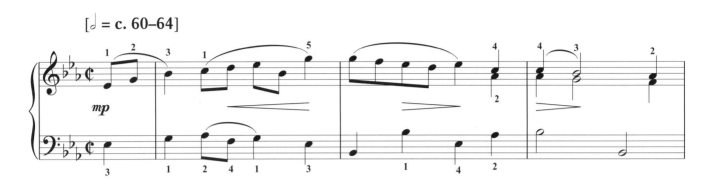

Minuet I
from French Suite No. 2 in C minor, BWV 813

Johann Sebastian Bach
(1685–1750)

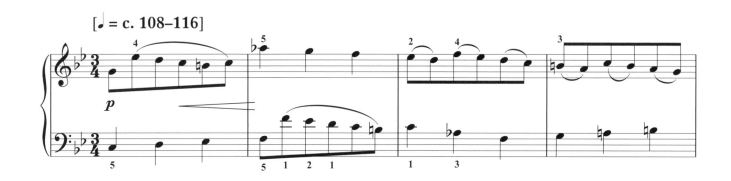

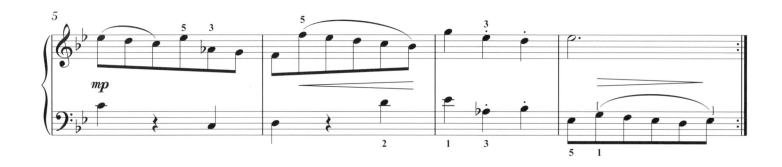

All slurs appear in the manuscript, except those in brackets, as do the staccatos in m. 7.

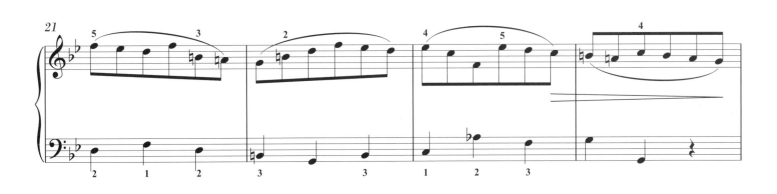

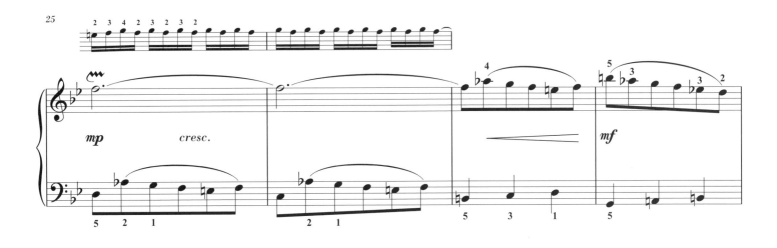

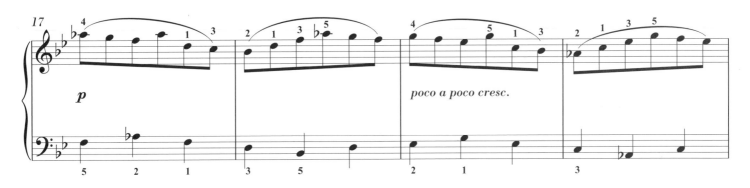

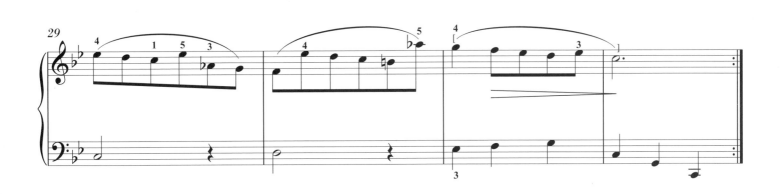

Minuet
from French Suite No. 6 in E Major, BWV 817

Johann Sebastian Bach

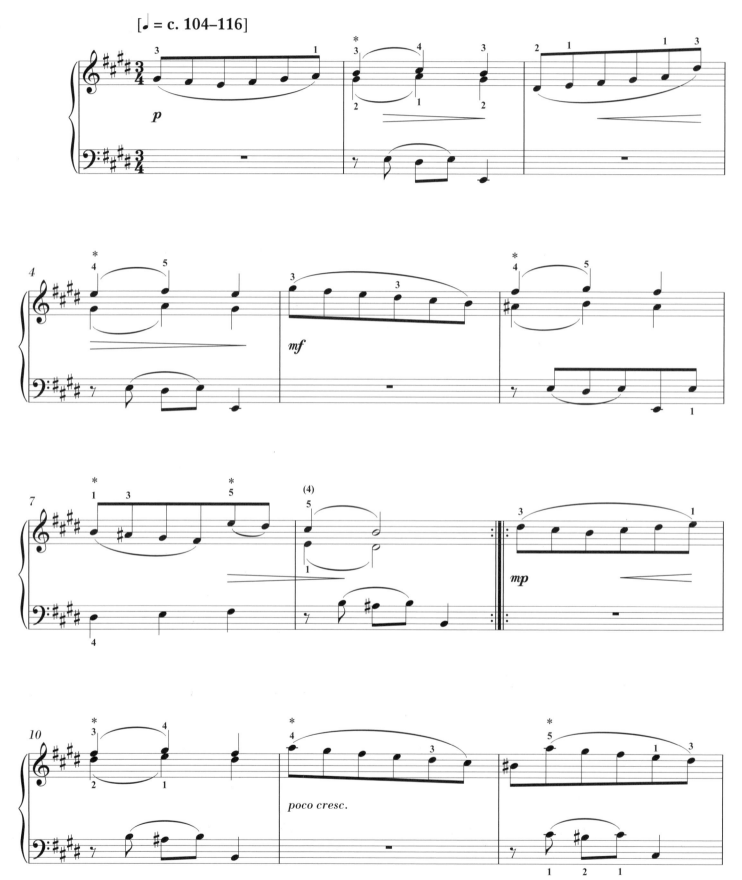

* These slur markings appear in the source manuscript.

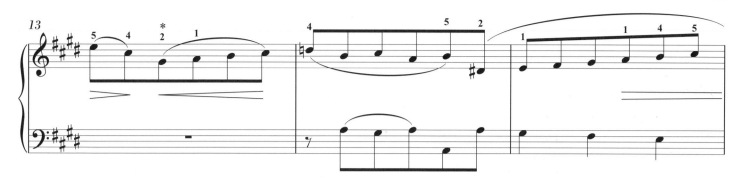

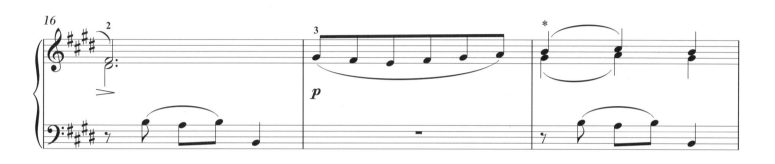

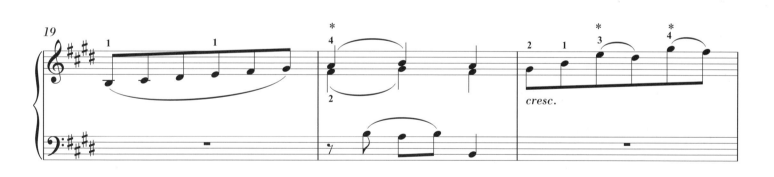

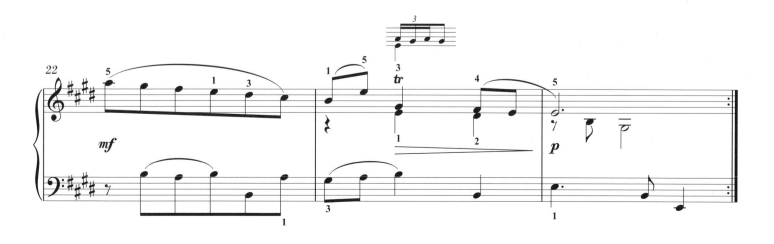

Minuet I
from Overture in G minor, BWV 822

Johann Sebastian Bach

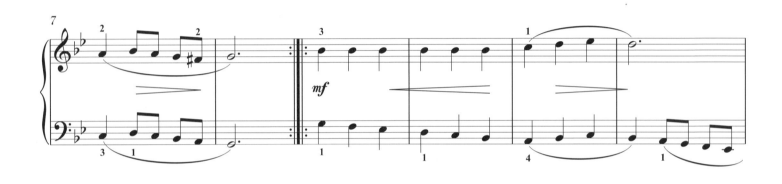

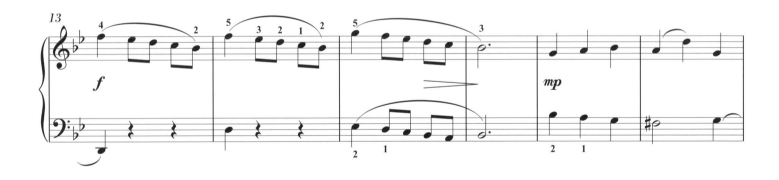

May perform all three Minuets from Overture in G minor as a group in the following order: 1–2–1–3–1.

Minuet II
from Overture in G minor, BWV 822

Johann Sebastian Bach

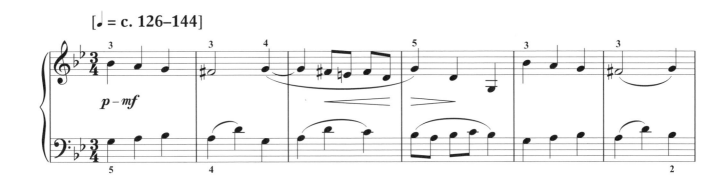

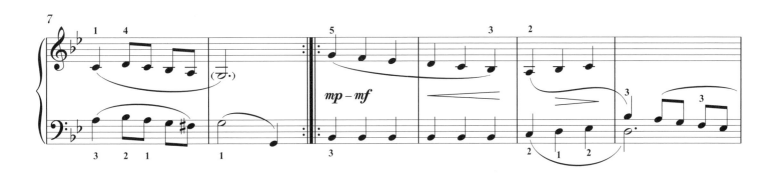

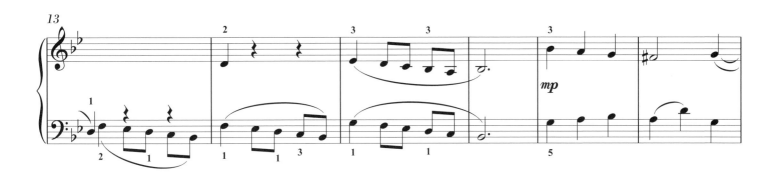

(Minuet 1 da capo)

Minuet 1 is on page 42.

Minuet III
from Overture in G minor, BWV 822

Johann Sebastian Bach

D.C.

Minuet in B-flat Major
BWV Appendix 118

Attributed to
Johann Sebastian Bach

[**Allegretto** ♩ = 100]

Minuet in G Major
BWV Appendix 116

Attributed to
Johann Sebastian Bach

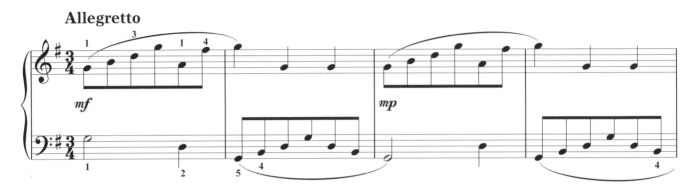

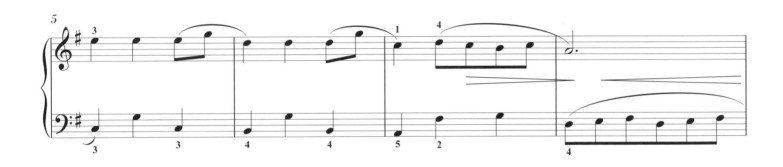

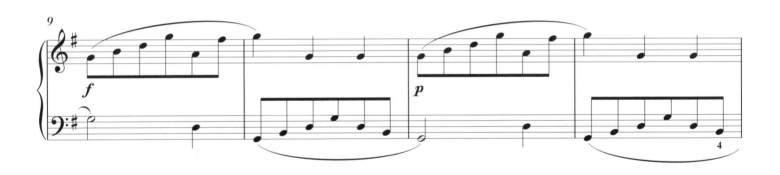

Fingerings, tempo, articulations, and dynamics are editorial suggestions.

Minuet in A Minor
BWV Appendix 120

Attributed to
Johann Sebastian Bach

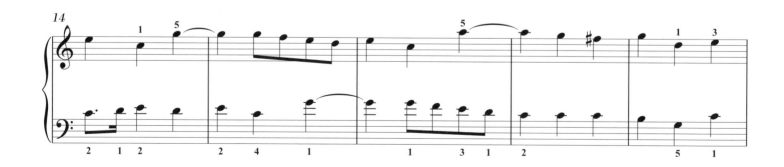

Minuet in C minor
BWV Appendix 121

Attributed to
Johann Sebastian Bach

Minuet in D minor
BWV Appendix 132

Attributed to
Johann Sebastian Bach

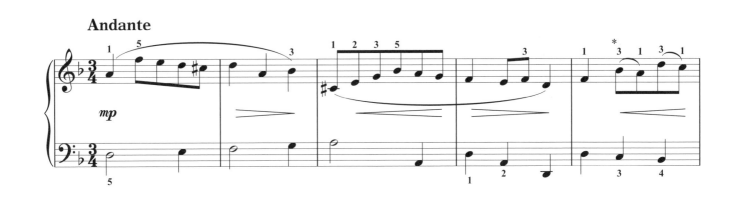

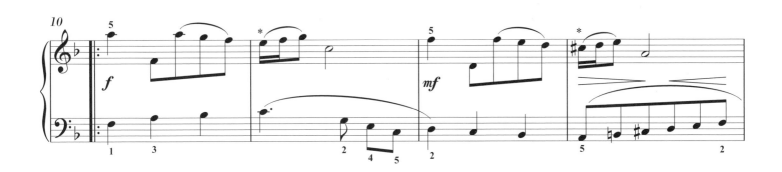

*These slurs appear in the source manuscript. Other slurs are editorial sugestions.
Tempo, articulations and dynamics are editorial suggestions.

Musette in D Major
BWV Appendix 126

Attributed to
Johann Sebastian Bach

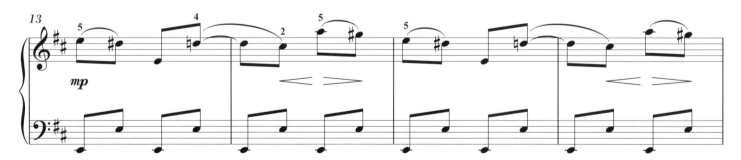

Fingerings, tempo, articulations and dynamics are editorial suggestions.

Musette
from English Suite No. 3 in G minor, BWV 808

Johann Sebastian Bach

* These two-note slurs appear in the source manuscript.

(Repeat Gavotte I)

O Haupt voll Blut und Wunden
(O Sacred Head, Now Wounded)
from *St. Matthew Passion*, BWV 244

Johann Sebastian Bach

Polonaise in F Major
BWV Appendix 117a

Attributed to
Johann Sebastian Bach

Polonaise in G minor

from *The Notebook for Anna Magdalena Bach*, BWV Appendix 119

Attributed to
Johann Sebastian Bach

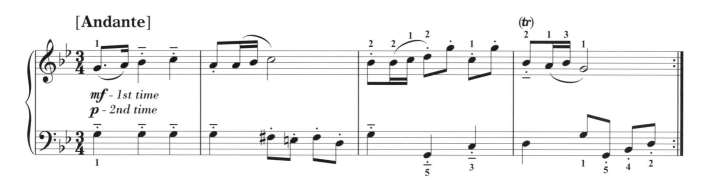

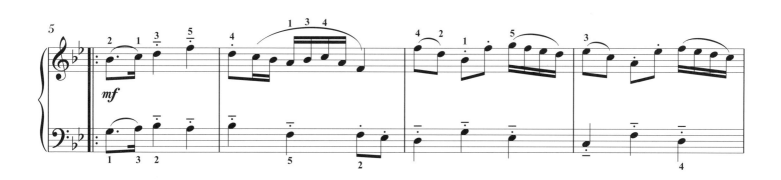

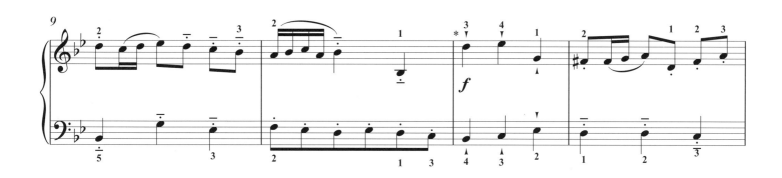

* These wedge markings in the right hand, indicating marcato, appear in the source manuscript. Other articulations, tempo and dynamics are editorial suggestions.

Polonaise in G Major
BWV Appendix 130

Johann Sebastian Bach

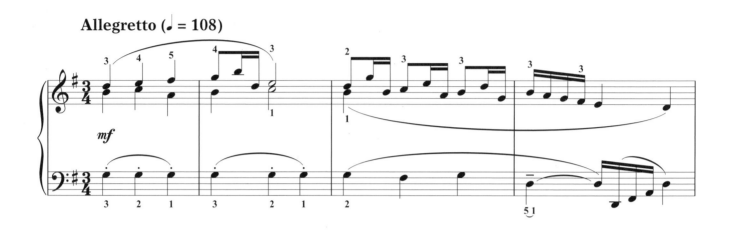

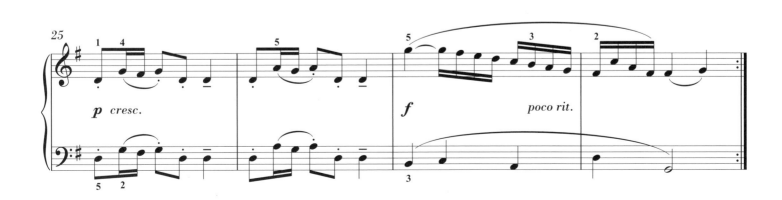

Prelude in C Major

BWV 924

Johann Sebastian Bach

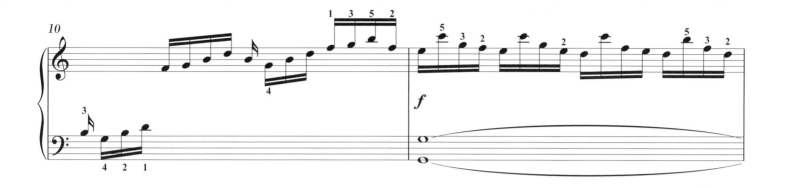

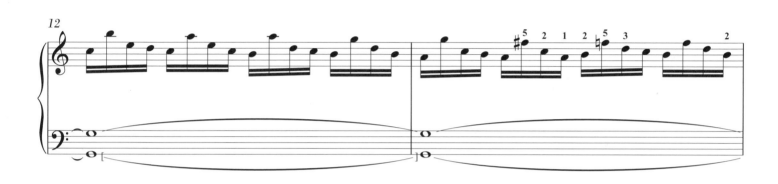

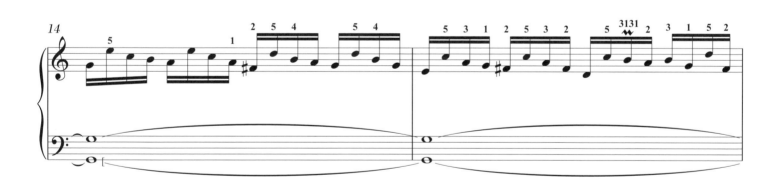

Prelude in D minor
BWV 926

Johann Sebastian Bach

Fingerings are editorial suggestions.

Prelude in F Major
BWV 927

Johann Sebastian Bach

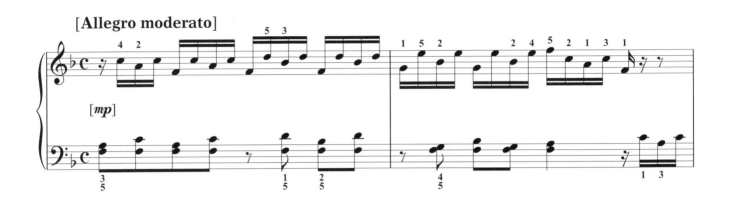

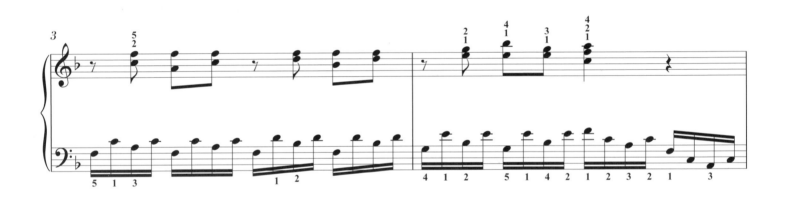

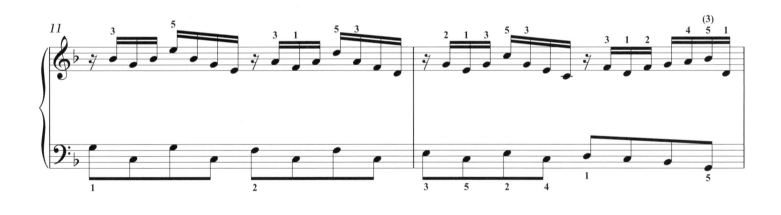

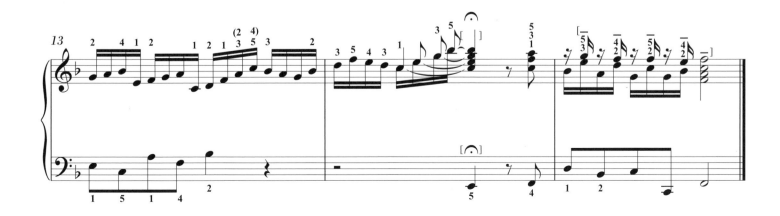

Prelude in G minor

BWV 930

Johann Sebastian Bach
(1685–1750)

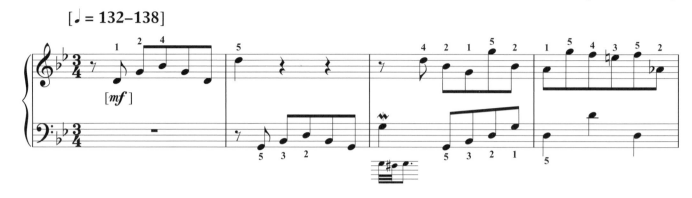

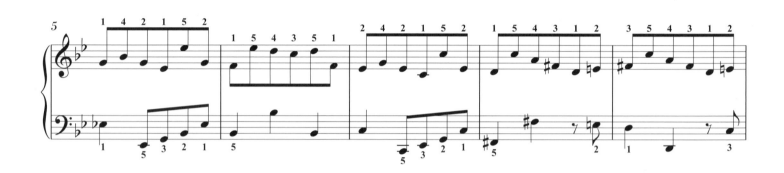

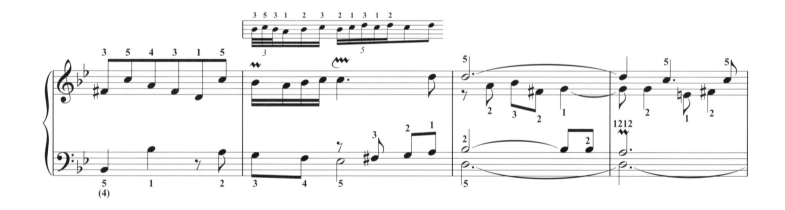

Prelude in C minor
BWV 934

Johann Sebastian Bach

Prelude in C Major

BWV 933

Johann Sebastian Bach
(1685–1750)

Prelude in C Major
BWV 939

Johann Sebastian Bach

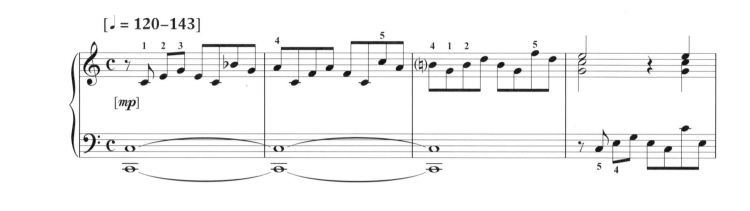

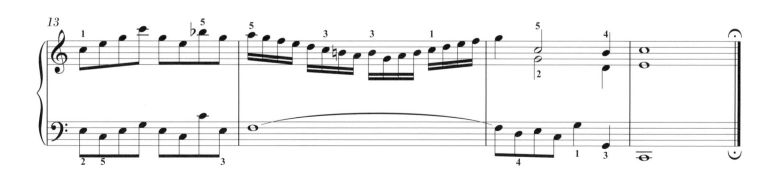

Prelude in D minor
BWV 940

Johann Sebastian Bach

Prelude in E minor
BWV 941

Johann Sebastian Bach
(1685–1750)

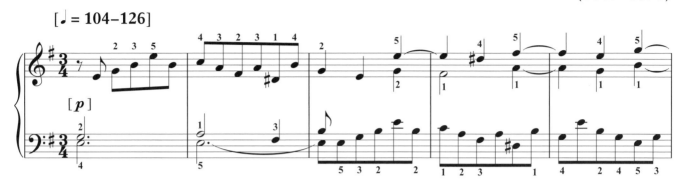

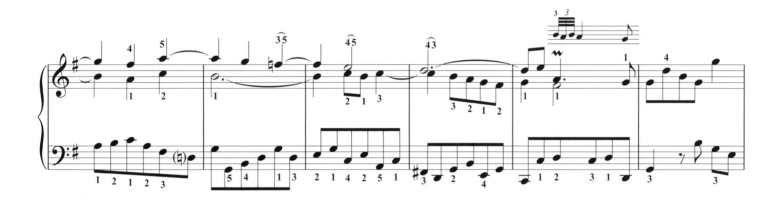

Prelude in A minor
BWV 942

Johann Sebastian Bach
(1685–1750)

Prelude in C minor

BWV 999

Johann Sebastian Bach

[Allegro moderato]

Fingerings are editorial suggestions.

Prelude in C Major

from *The Well-Tempered Clavier*, Book I, BWV 846

Johann Sebastian Bach

Toccata and Fugue in D minor
BWV 565

Johann Sebastian Bach

FUGUE

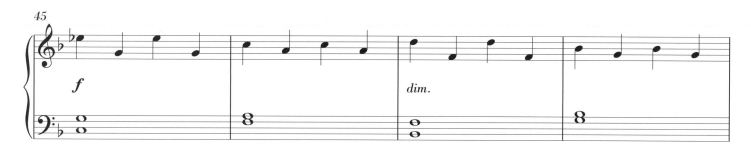

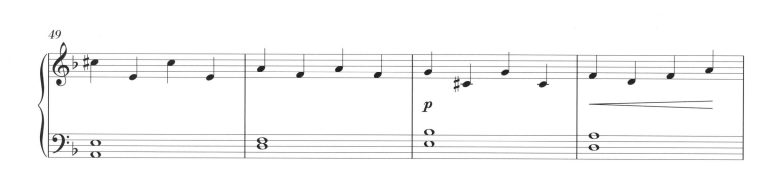

Sarabande
from English Suite No. 2 in A minor, BWV 807

Johann Sebastian Bach

[Andante sostenuto]

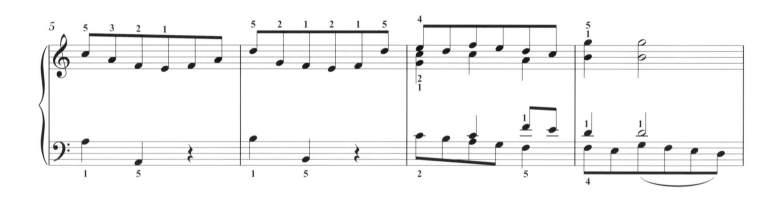

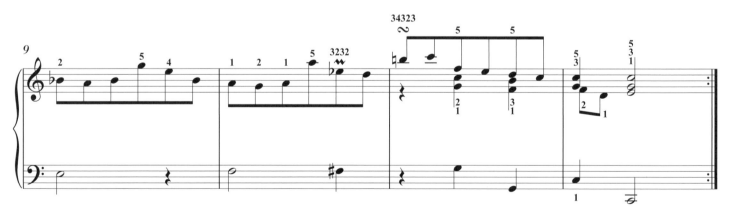

This piece has been revoiced for ease of reading for an intermediate pianist.

Sarabande
from English Suite No. 5 in E minor, BWV 810

Johann Sebastian Bach

* These two slurs are indicated in the source manuscript.

Sheep May Safely Graze
from Cantata BWV 208

Johann Sebastian Bach

Sleepers, Awake

from *Wachet auf, ruft uns die Stimme*, BWV 140

Johann Sebastian Bach

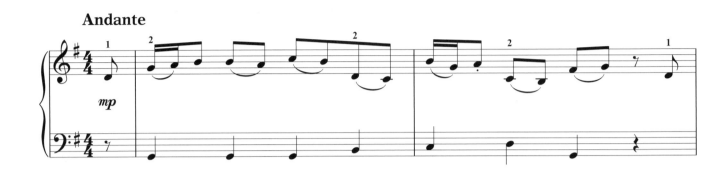